Imperfection
in a
Perfect World

By Roberto Carlos Martinez

PublishAmerica
Baltimore

ISBN: 1-4241-9170-X
PUBLISHED BY PUBLISHAMERICA, LLLP
www.publishamerica.com
Baltimore

Printed in the United States of America

This work of poetry is a journey into the minds of a generation that wants to be heard, and at times refuses to believe what it is told but instead decides for themselves what truth is. A group of people who know that the ability to change the world is in their hands. A generation that will not only change the way we look at prejudice, politics, racism, family and depression, but the way we look at the world.

For my cousin, Christopher Alcides Parada, who grew up in front of my eyes and whose childhood helped me understand many things about life and myself.

FIRE

Introduction

I am going to write a poem.

Beautiful as the Resplendent Quetzal.
Painful as the eyes of the suffering.
Dry as a dead sea.

I will write a poem.

Tough as life itself.
Cheerful as childhood memories.

No…wait…
Let me rethink that.

I will write a book.

About a world,
The things we cannot say,
The things we are afraid to say.

About the importance of being you.

Of those who have failed to speak,
of those hidden from the world,
of those who were told it was wrong to feel this way or that way.

Let me write a book about that world.

Amorously

Polka-dotted butterfly arrives from heaven, clinging to the nearby tree.
Inspecting the nearby city, it senses the fear in the human world,
and releases the love hidden under its fragile wings.

Thoughts

They take over this frigid body.
Tightly wrapping themselves around every stiff limb
and every bloody organ,
spreading the dead vines through me.
I become cold clay.

Emotionless.
Only silent death in the feeling itself.

Melted smiles running down every wrinkle on my face.
The light that fades with every tear unshed.

I remember.
How I clung to the wall, spread myself against it.
Returning to that cold state.

Where voices passed by me like pictures on a white canvas.
Refusing to return to me.

I've scared myself back into my rusted cage.
To think about the world.

Sweet

The rusted seat of defeat awaits my arrival.
Those who let go of my hand, eagerly waited for this moment.

For me to violently crash under failure.
I become a dry leaf…crunchy, hard and even more fragile than before.

Cold dry days reminding of desert air.
When hunger for happiness has frozen over like a drop of water in
the coldest winter day.

They laugh at what they don't understand like a jack-in-the-box
whose only purpose is to jump out.
Their noses turn red fire and their clothes take the color of ignorance.

One day, they may understand.
Those spider webs inside their ears will melt
and allow them to listen clearly.
Their brains will become soft like pillows, and they will think.

Feel

Repressed emotions waiting to let go of what was unclear.
Waiting to be set free, clawing at fear itself.
The inner self...
afraid, afraid.

A Being

A beautiful being falls from heaven.
Not knowing where or when the journey will end.

A beautiful being falls from heaven.
A perfect vessel of love,
who has no self distinction of what is race nor color.

Breath

Heavenly-given love.
Filling it with filth and our own prejudices.
Demolishing what was once pure.

Clear

Colossal buildings overshadow what was once in peace under the sky.
What our ancestors had fought for forever vanished.

Beauty, folded like aged skin.
Life taken as if it has no purpose.

Sorrow

Sorrow is an abrasive reality creeping through the front door.
Silently hiding in the corners of the walls,
taking the soft shape of those inside it.
Suddenly we set out to breathe it.
Slowly suffocating us into a feeling of worthlessness

Sitting in the bare middle of the cold room, I stare at the walls,
waiting for the solution to sneak in.

Death

Have you encountered death within me?
Whispering in the darkness of a new moon.
The glimmering sadness confuses many.

It fiercely flutters, deep inside of me.
Spreading it's ember-like wings, agitating my anima.

Waiting to drag me into the dull earth
to return to the place I should have never left.

Afterwards, its wondrous wings will take flight once again,
to the flesh of another.

Bad Day

I awoke to the soft melancholic beating of my cherry-red heart.
The sensation tangling me into the reality I so refuse.
The waves slamming me over the hot dry sand.

It arrived like a box seeded with evils, never meant to be opened.

I had a bad day.
Blossoming flowers, crystalline candies,
they burned crisply into the fire.
I felt the anguish, pure restlessness, the defeat.

A tornado screamed inside me and shattered my deep glass shell.
I ran, like a dog on fire.

The Soul

The soul has long hunted for peace in the despair of the world.
Searching for the light that penetrates the sea.
Walking on a clear blue ocean, floating onto a white puffy cloud,
and eventually learning to fly.
Then, it untangles itself from hatred.

Dark Angel

Mentally ill me sits in the black chair next to the black angel.
I ponder what faith must feel like.
I take the veil that protected me all my life.

And I give in to my destiny.

Alone

I study the old decay that has long spread inside me.
Into the coldly lit blue room, bathing myself in the pool of blood.

I take a shower to take away the stress, the mutilating sadness.

Loneliness sits there like a cat waiting for food,
meowing at me with its deadly lips.
Staring and imitating my every move.

Only when I recognize it's there do I understand my reality.

Living

I wonder what it must be like to wake up furious at the world.
Angry at those around you.
Absorbing the lives out of loved ones, like a hateful putrid sponge.

Inside.
Perhaps only rotten decay, shaded with black moss.
Must be the smell of early death.

If one day there was guilt for the pain caused, what would it feel like?
Like the brushing of the wind on your hand
or like the sound of a pin falling on glass?
Or maybe guilt is the last stage before the death
of those who have fallen in the darkness.

Power

The young one you tore down.
Took every moist leaf and every breathing branch.

Left the barren death of me and then burned what was left.

I still hurt.
I still feel.
The war still lives inside of me.

Wonderful

Many times the smile fades, running into eager sadness.
You run, back into the old pearl.

The whispers felt through every cell.
The tears heard running under the skin.

The storm ends and the smile resurrects.

Uncongenial

Sullen voices softly speak to me.
Empty gaping holes waiting to devastate me.

Words had suspended meanings, touch had felt it take over.

Beautiful loneliness encases me.
I am a frigid empty room waiting to be filled.
Footsteps of happiness, only memories.
Time no longer spins me into reality.

I refuse to give in.
I roll up into a small and suddenly intense glass orb.
Shift back into me, the hollow solitary rock.

Where I hide, waiting for them to find me.

The Untitled Poem

The light no longer enters my dark room
Sparkling diamonds have metamorphosed into black coal.
I try to hear their voices telling me to rise once again.
But it's been so long since I saw the light.

Darkness swallows me, only empty space in my eyes.

There are insects all over the wall.
There are scars all over my soul.
My blood spills from my heart.

I don't want to feel this way, don't need drugs.
I won't let it get me down.
It is in me, not in the world.

Brother

Friends who had our warm-hearted moments.
Clueless enemies.
I am cognac, you're liquor.

You are my hero in times of failure, love in times of frustration,
and truth in times of doubt.

Understand.
We calmly swim together down the river.
If you crash onto the concrete floor like a glass chandelier, I fail.
If you reach the happiness that you have always searched for, I win.
For one fruit depends on all the others in a basket.

I am a tiger, you are the stripes that adorn me.

Family Tree

What are they doing to me?
Withdrawing the water from my lips, sunlight from my eyes,
and I only feeding off shade.

The guiding hand forces me away.
I drink from the foreign river, take a taste from the forbidden silence.

Never to return to the tree from which I flourished.
Fruits bore from the same tree, not having the same taste.
I fight to never be like them, like the stars and clouds fighting for the sky.

It Lies Dormant

After many years I see you again.
"Do you remember?" you ask.
"Yes, I remember," I say.

I go into the silent place.
Into the sour past, sleeping but aching.

I remember.
Where you had hurt me so many times.
My childhood.
The time you hit me with so much anger.
The belt, a reflection of you.

Today you awoke that feeling.
I stood silent for a couple of minutes.
The bruises resurfaced on my skin; wet blood and angry swelling.

Guardian

You would drink my blood if you could.
Traitor, bad friend.
Liar, bad blood.
Serpent, just waiting to spread your venom.
Poisonous tarantula.
Slow walker, fast killer.
You would trap me in your web if you could.
Never taking the blame, forever wanting to be the victim.
Faker, it's in your face.
Liar, it's in your soul.

Mother

From a lighted faraway place, I danced my way into your womb
where I would lay to rest until the time was right.

I felt the sadness of the world inside of me.
You introduced happiness into my little heart and allowed
wisdom to seep into my skin.

When I arrived, they did speak of me.
But they knew nothing.
But you knew.

You knew who I was.
One, we once were.

Reflection

The innocence of cupid lies in you.
At times I see you cry in despair
like death has just walked through the door.
At times I hear you laugh like life was meant for you.
Other times I hear you scream like someone I do not know.

It hurts to know that you are only a victim of this cruel world like a
fly around food or a mosquito feeding.

For you are only a victim of life,
like a forest near an overpopulated area.

The Mentality

The secret of the men who fling their bills
to the women who are in need.
The secret of the men who fling their bills
to the children who have nothing.
The guilty extortion of the innocent.

Numbers, sexual objects.
Insulting what was once sacred.

A fantasy that goes beyond morals.
Shame.
Buying the bodies of others.

The victims, no longer look at someone in the eyes.
Lose their self worth.
This is what is done to make one feel good.

Don't pretend it's not there, it has long been happening.

But it is the excited ones who come and pay.
Business men, politicians, husbands and many more.

Don't pretend it's not there, it has long been happening.
The result of those who take advantage of extreme poverty.

Gloom

The intoxication takes you over and you collapse down on the
muddy soil like a watermelon, killing silence.
It stirs me deep inside until I melt to the sound of your failure.
Hearing the voice I no longer recognize
fading out of every cell in your body.

What I can do, only you know.
I am a faraway whisper.

Nestlings

Hold me tightly, without causing me pain.
Caress me with your inner touch.
Let me be the smile in your love and dreams.
For now.

Teach me how to fly like the birds of paradise.
Wind, give me strength of independence.
Let the bud open and take life in, branches extend and the leaves grow.

When I need the space, let me grow.
Let me know safety.
Feed me safety not fear.

With freedom, I expand.
In a cage, I die.

I will tumble under the waves, find my way in a forest.
I will rise because of love.

Angel's Lament

The white spring rose, awaiting release, sitting there on the bed.
Your loving wings dangling over your shoulders.

Where many sorrowful tears have dried out.
Where no one sees you.

The strong emotions have long awakened within you.
You dream of him, hoping to feel him again.
I see the smile in your sadness.

Sad angel, don't cry.
Raise your wings, allow the wind to reclaim them.
They were made to fly.

Love hurts today,
tomorrow it will all be okay.

Forgive Me

Forgive me.
Forgive the rose for being a rose.
Forgive the tree for bearing branches.

Forgive me.
Forgive me for being myself, not what you wanted.
It wasn't a choice, it was destined.

Forgive me.
For you are a rose.
And I…
I am the thorns that grew next to it.

Rage

I twist and turn with the hectic strength of the earth's core,
renewing myself, rising.

Flames of bloody red and citrus orange consume me.
Becoming rage and truth ablaze.

I jump on a white cloud to see if I still exist.
Melting onto its whiteness.

Comrades

The will to take a knife for them is not enough,
for they would be willing to tear it into your skin.

You're just another body, a piece of flesh like what they eat.

Sincere

There are times when I become gentle and tender,
soft as a tiny ball of cotton.
I stick myself to you, so you can feel the despair in me.
There is sadness in my struggle, happiness in my solitude.

I become real, you can touch me.
I take the shape of a wingless bird, a colorless chameleon.
I take the color of an apple an hour after it has been cut.
I take the smell of an autumn leaf under the rain.
I release myself.
I release myself.
I release myself from the thick rusted muddy ropes tying me to my past.

Confess

It hurts as much as it hurts a piece of paper to burn in the flames.
To see you, the victim I did not see, turning to drugs.

All smiles in the beginning.
Just for fun, just for fun.
Almost overnight, your smile consumed by the black smoke and alcohol.

The need to be happy, found in what could only hurt you.

Watching you...
I wish I could forget everything.
The sullen sleepless nights, piercing screams, and cursed tears
flowing through my mind.

Pages

I will hear your laughter as the pages of my life burn.
As I lose myself in the barbarous sadness of life.

Only to rise once again, losing myself in divine faith.

Run

The other cheek I turned, waiting for harmonious love
and heartfelt sympathy.
Two cheeks were not enough.

I slowly made an inner commitment to fall apart.
Melting into defeat.

I gained the concealed knowledge and I released the skill in me.

Kite

Small adventurous boy raised his kite to the wind.
Did not know what destiny had hidden for him.

An aluminum can wrapped with string on his right hand.
His left hand releasing or letting go.

Little boy with the luminous smile who did not know
three shots would end a future that was never promised.

On that hot summer day, when almost a man, it happened.
Surprised not by the sound of bullets but by the pain of them on his back.
He grabbed onto the metal pole to show he was a fighter.
There he died under a hot sun, leaning against that pole,
with a pool of blood caressing him.

The young one who killed him,
a victim himself who had once felt remorse.

The One

His scars are called rebellion, it's freedom.
He wears defeat, to see who his enemies are.

He grabs a knife, to see if he still bleeds.

Older

I am older,
but the feeling still lives there; in the corner of the red sky.
It burns my skin, seeping into my veins.

I am older,
but it doesn't change; the peace of mind.

Life is like that.
We get stuck in mid-air, out of breath.
Somehow, we find a way to live with it.

Giving up would be cowardly.
Living with it would be courageous.

I came into the world with the soul of a dove.
As if a great wave of love had slammed into me
and left me senseless.

One day, I awoke from my mystifying sleep, and I understood
what the books had failed to put into words.
What wisdom we had once denied.

The Struggle

They set a nightmare for us.
The illusion of goals and no reward.
Every day struggling to be them.

But if we were them,
our hearts would probably be as minuscule as theirs.

The fools, run to them.
Fall for that song of religion.
It's their best weapon.

Their influence becomes bigger, but ours smaller.
But their hearts…
Their hearts will probably burn in the fire.

If

When you fall into the painful nightmare
of those on the other side of the world,
You question why, or what you are doing there.
In that disillusioned desert land, that has long fed on the bloodshed.

The yearning to write to Mother and tell her how much you love her.
The unification of the beginning and the end.

"If" I return, things will be different you say.

What

Sadly witnessing the blood escaping from the wounds of the innocent,
I see a distinct pain living in the eyes of the children,
and permanent suffering awakening in the hearts of mothers.

I feel the rage of a billion shattered glass pieces, the betrayal of Judas,
and the death of martyrs.

I drown in the ageless longing for home.
What I must do, I do not know, I can only try.

There is no clue of what awaits near the end.

You can only hope "they" understand.
You hope "they" understand what they cannot see.

Sacrifices

Shattered dreams of life.
Empty wooden crosses.
Nightmares of reality.

Fire

There are times when they encase me.
In between those walls, in their boxes.
The deception of what is healing but only defeating.

They teach me to detest what I see in the mirror.
They set the dark colors for me, the hidden lies.

But when I get out, I become unearthly.
I become a flame dancing on paper boxes.
I play the risk they refuse to be.
I get out of that burden binding me from fulfillment.
I tell you, it's about passion.
The passion to be yourself.

EARTH

Share

I'll share my lips with you.
For they are soft, tender, and easy to surrender.
Share your loneliness with me, the only thing that makes you love me.

If I look away, don't be alarmed.
I just have to distract my sight, from those brown eyes I refuse to lie to.

For Me

If after making love…
Silence swallows me like a marshmallow in a fire.
Don't ask "what are you thinking?"
There are things meant only for me.

For my mind is the only thing the world cannot dominate.

Heal

Speak to me and take the part of me that heals
and hangs from the fruitful tree.
Kiss me and take the part of me that hurts.
That burns like a flower in fire.

What Could Be

It's the autumn in your brown eyes that confuses me.
You whisper to me your longings, dreams and what we could be.

But I have dreams that have nothing to do with commitment.

Speechless, I sit quietly, but I do not lie.

Don't Worry

If I melt onto your picture like plastic in fire, it's just me being stupid.
If I look into your brown eyes and I look confused,
it's just me being stupid.

If I love, it's just me being stupid.

If the truth hurts...don't worry.

Question

It's the face that I see in the mirror that you love.
It's my way of letting you take over that pleases you.

But at times I become the beast.
And I hurt you like a dry leaf in the snow.
I tear you, later realizing I am sorry.

I turn my back on your "sorry," to get you back.
I get you back for those times you left me there.
For all those times I was the stupid one.
Is this love?

Contradictions

Today I leave you.
Tomorrow you return for me.

In your absence, you become nothing.
When you return, you bring a storm of love.
And I bring you an earthquake of sadness.

See

Let me finally see.
What I could not see before.
I got a problem, perhaps an obsession.
For loving you, for holding you.

I count the lines on your hands.
Yet, you're so young and I feel much older.

But the pain, it drives itself throughout my body.
And my dreams they melt onto yours.

To Learn

It is the heart that learns to lose, the heart that learns to win.
The heart that knows what could be and what cannot.

Red bloody veins, needles, and sour words…I could not forget.
I had to learn, I had to learn.

Brown eyes had never shined for me that way.
Small lips, I had never tasted them like that.

Those months we were together, it was you who I
looked for when the phone rang.
It was you who filled me up with words of commitment.

But I knew, but I knew.
I had to let you go.

You said "you left me for another."
But I knew.
What you could not understand.

For small minds believe you must always be with someone,
and smart minds know we are not all destined to do that.
For destiny told me to leave you.
And my heart had to understand what my mind could not.

"You will never forget me for I will always be in your heart
and you in mine," you said.

In my heart, I wonder.
Was this the one?

Understand

If at night I hear you whisper my name.
It's because I love you.
If at night I search for you in my dreams.
It's because I love you.

Let your loving words fulfill my fantasies.
Let a whisper from you make me melt like butter in a pan.

When we were together, many times you whispered, "I love you."
But I had to doubt it.
I had to ignore it even when I felt it.
And one day you will understand why.

Walk Away

Mi amor.
My hard-headed love.
Let me walk away from you.

Let me walk away from the heartbreak you will cause later on.
Allow me to see reality, the real you.

I leave you empty handed.
I take with me, nothing.
Just the memories of you wrapped in an envelope.

Listen

Have you searched in my heart before?
Have you felt what I feel?

If only you listened.
If only you stopped being selfish.

Listen.
Listen.
To what I feel.
To what satisfies me.

Feed me love, not desire.
Feed me truth, not half-lies.

Be there for me.
Be there for me when I need love.

I need love.
I need love.
Not sex.

Worth

You speak to my heart.
Your lips follow the beat of mine.
Your innocent smile declares its love to me.

You bring out the little boy in me.
The one who's not afraid to love, you're the red in the rose
and green in the leaves.

"Only with me okay," you say.

And only with you do thoughts seem stupid.
Love seems worth it?

I Am Sorry

My love
Many times I waited for you.

Sitting there, waiting for that day to come.
When it came, you delayed it.

And I waited like a fool.

And one day you smiled at me.
And said, "I am sorry."

Over

Destiny is what keeps us apart.
And you used me, I used you.

For loneliness brought us together.
When one of us lost that, it was over.

You Had Not Called

I called.
I heard that voice.
From deep within that device.

And it told me.
It repeated to me that you had returned.

But you had not called.
But you had not called.

For you had forgotten.
You had something else.

Two Weeks

The love you declared to me.
So many times you repeated those words to me.
I always had to be strong.

In the end, two weeks erased that.
And you fell in love with another.

Song

For this powerful emotion many have fallen.
In the timeless need to want to be with someone.
The missing piece to all our flaws.

It becomes powerful enough to give up our dreams.

Today I drew a map of love.
The great expectations of what it should be.
But at times it weathers, at times it's rough.

Today I wrote a song about a loved one; delicate and intimate.
But the ones we love sometimes do not understand.

Years go by, still not over it.
Forget it and go on.

Investing time, precious empty time.

Love, like in stories, such a hopeful thing.

Into

Orange shaded sky
over a white canvas heart
slide into my soul.

Simple Words

A rain of words fell into the desert of my heart.

Hiding with you by my side.
Where the warmth takes me over once more.
I am like the sun, like the crescent shape of the moon.
Leaping onto a leaf carried by the breeze.

My love.
Let those simple words be like warm whispers under water,
sonant smiles in the dark,
or a tender winder breeze.

If I love today, will I live tomorrow?
If I leave, will I see you once more?
If I listen, will I melt onto your heart and soul?

Earth

I dance in the soil of my ancestors.
What they stole from us and what we could have been.

I dance in the soil of my ancestors, though they may be buried,
we are not defeated.
Their undefeated courage, compassionate love,
and ego-less pride extends through me.
Breathing through every cell, swimming through every vein.

I dance in the soil of my ancestors.
I dance for them.
For those who were true.
For those who never gave up.
For those whose wisdom seeped through me.

I dance in the soul of my ancestors for I am them and they are me.
I dance.
I dance.
For one day my children will dance too.

WIND

Jar

You arrived amid a summer sunshine on a day when I did not
understand who you were.
Your smile slithered into my eyes and your voice breezed into my ears.
"I love you," you said.

Here

I need to be here.
I need to be here.

With you in this unmeasured moment.

I want to pay attention to your heart beating.
Even if it's for the last time.

Lie

If you can't trust me.
Then how can I love you?
How do I speak to what only sees me
but does not listen?

Welcome

Forgive the heart that harbors in the shade.
The heart that did not consider love.
Forgive the heart that endowed in fear.

For it is the fear that sends true love away.

Forgive it.
Forgive the tears it drowns in.
Forgive the eyes clouded in red.

Perhaps

To find you now.
It hurts me so.

I asked for love.
The wish was granted.

But I did not know.
I did not know.

The pain it would cause me.

The road where I would carry you.
Only to lose you.
Only to lose you.

For perhaps that road was the path to heaven.

Bruise

Many times I wanted to end it.
For you were hurting me.
But above all, I was hurting myself.

Many times I picked up that silent phone.
When I dialed, I heard your sweet voice.

That sound would travel to my heart
and my heart would soften once more.

I could not leave you.

What would I do without you?
Was I denying what was given to me?

Numb

Once I broke your heart.
Twice you won my love.

At times I did not know what I was doing.
But deep inside I knew things weren't the way they looked.

For the pain still lived there.
The doubts and memories left of the other ones.

Just Us

In the morning I love you like a flower loves sunlight.
At night I become the sun and you the moon.

But it is those later days.
Those later days in which I can't have enough.

I wish we had a place.
I wish we had independence.

Passing

The rain falls over my eternal loss.
The sun no longer shines in my garden.
My world holds your silence.

Only Us

Nothing would matter.
Nothing would matter if you were here.
Shaded under the light in my blue room.

Stir

When I feel lonely, the heat of your body grows inside of me.
Awakening the residue of you.

I begin to miss you.

Mind

Listen to the things that change deep inside.
Where patience has long waited for you.

Harmonious

I find refuge in your rainy smile.
I encounter peace in your earthy eyes.
I discover love in your human words.

Tonight

My love,
you stayed with me tonight
under the burning candlelight of my soul.

Is

Don't say a word when I kiss you.
Let the taste take over me.

Wind

Find a way through every obstacle.
See the reality in life.

Caress the barricades in your way.
Don't let them defeat you.
Show them love, for it's not what they know.

WATER

The Light

Smile when you feel angry enough to make the walls bleed.
Laugh when you feel sad enough to leave it all behind.
You are like the rays of the sun, for only you know your limits.

Green prairies, blue skies, and eternal light await you.
When things get gray, consume them.
Let yourself be the light.
Love the best you can.
Remember that you are the mountain.
Many arrive there and many will return with nothing.

Benevolent

Falling into the warmth of the dark-lighted room,
I saw you sitting there on the fluffy white sofa.

You raised the guitar like a third hand you had hidden.
You smiled at me with your dark tender eyes
and your heavenly honey smile.
Slowly you captivated me with the beauty of a red rose and the
fragileness of a two-lobed stigma of a red bush monkey flower.

Staring into your angelic face, we allowed our eyes to converse.

As you began to play, my soul took the shape of your guitar.
My eyes followed the movements of your fingers,
the peace in your talent.
Then I heard your tranquil voice escaping from your soft lips.
A mature voice vocalizing beyond your years.
Thinking with your heart as the words flowed from your soul.

Minutes later, you placed the guitar next to you
with the most devoted emotion.

Dilemma

From the moment of my first breath.
I feel you here.

Like silence that is unheard but felt.
Like love that lives but is hidden.
And like the closest love.
I don't recognize you.

Even if time draws us further apart.
The memories live deep inside me.
Like red blood, running with the most dazzling beauty.

The Peak

The ones who never spoke the truth see themselves in you.
They faithlessly adorn themselves in darkness
pretending to know the truth.

When at the peak, you look down.
Dogs, fighting for an oily tortilla.

Little by little they will defeat you and stab you in your soul.

But you already know.
What was hidden, discovered it.
What they would say in whispers, you heard it long ago.

In your heart you know the truth.
What they say or think, it doesn't matter.

You know the truth.
The one who believes in the truth will never be defeated by lies.
Because the peak is not on earth.

Angel of Death

It came to me during that final night.
I had never seen anything like it.
A silk white robe it wore, held a scythe on its left hand.

I froze at the sight of its enormous white wings.
The sight of them, as if they carried life itself.

It stared into my frightened eyes and reached its right hand to me.
I silently gave my good hand away.

"It's okay," it said.
"I am here."

The Dream

I thought I heard you whisper my name
like the resonance of a seashell being dragged into the sea.

In that reoccurring dream.
Where I catch a glimpse of you sitting by the cliff.
Waiting for me, in the shadows of the night, surrounded by the
hollow trees, watching over you before my arrival.

As I get close, I think I hear a knocking at my brain.
A type of migraine or worm waiting for me to awake.

When the moon descends in front of you
like a companion who has known you all along,
I see the light I could not see before.

I walk over to you.
As I am about to embrace you, you begin to turn around.
You silently gaze at me, as you see my white wings release
themselves into your field of view.

Experience

Mother, bear in mind.
The individual who made you smile.
The obedient and blessed me.
The one you sheltered from the addictions of the world.

I learned, Mother.
I began to nourish my starving spirit.
My wings grew and they led me to heaven.

There I found I had to be free and I found I had to be true to my heart.
I had to aid others like the tree that protects others in shade.

You never could understand that.
To you, family was number one.
To you, only family existed.

I read, I heard and I meditated.
I learned that all of us on this earth are a family.

Find

A generation of insecurities hangs onto the rope
of the tree that once was strong.
How to teach their children to be strong, they do not know.
Wisdom and self love, they never learned it.

There are times when mistakes bring maturity and there are times
when mistakes only bring more insecurities.

Hearing a mother say "I can't raise my child."
She is not using her head nor her heart.
She may just be selfish or perhaps confused.
For a mother is willing to take whatever comes her way.

As the years fly, generations of children who are insecure.

Insecurity is a weakness that must be fought.
If weak today, be stronger tomorrow.
Don't let others make up an image of perfection.

Let love guide you.
Always be yourself, wisely.
Change when you need to.
But never look too far away from where you were.
If you forget where you come from, you may get lost.
Follow the tracks of your ancestors, for it is your duty to finish them.

Listen to the heart that gives you strength.
Turn your ears away from those who say "you can't do it."
Turn your ears away from those who say "why haven't you done this?"
Take your time.
For we all have a destiny.
Some flowers are red, some are yellow, and some are white.

If at times you look in a magazine and see beauty don't say
"I wish I was like them."
They may be less happy than you.

If at times you doubt yourself, always remember…you are faith.
It is you who chooses to lose or be lost.

Never fear the life that disrupts your sleep.
Fear who they want you to be, not who you are.

But above all…love yourself.

Water

Many times I wish I could shatter into a million pieces.
Maybe that would take the pain away.
Maybe that way, my love would spread everywhere...
in order to erase hate.